Spot the difference
ANIMALS!

© 2022 Webber Books

All rights reserved. This book or any portion thereof may not be reproduced or used in any manner whatsoever without the express written permission of the publisher except for the use of brief quotations in a book review.

FIND 5 Differences!

FIND 5 Differences!

Brr! This is a cold place for animals to live!

Can you spot the 8 DIFFERENCES...?

FIND **6** DIFFERENCES!

FIND 6 Differences!

The cute cats have taken over the living room!

Can you spot the 9 DIFFERENCES...?

FIND 6 Differences!

FIND 7 Differences!

These sisters run a lovely little **animal farm!**

Can you spot the 9 DIFFERENCES...?

FIND 7 Differences!

FIND 7 Differences!

Aww! Cats and dogs make such great **pets**!

FIND
7
Differences!

FIND 7 differences!

It's a **very warm day** out here in the desert!

Can you spot the 9 DIFFERENCES...?

FIND 7 Differences!

FIND 8 Differences!

You'll find **lots** of animals living in this **forest**!

Can you spot the 9 DIFFERENCES...?

FIND 10 Differences!

FIND 10 DIFFERENCES!

ANSWERS!

ANSWERS!

Thanks for playing!